S0-AGC-348

This book belongs to

Thaydée,

a little Leo.

The Five Mile Press Pty Ltd
1 Centre Road, Scoresby
Victoria 3179 Australia
www.fivemile.com.au
Part of the Bonnier Publishing Group
www.bonnierpublishing.com

Cataloguing-in-publication data is available for this book

This edition first published 2014

Copyright © Camilla Gracanin, 2014
Illustrations by Thea Baker
Design copyright © The Five Mile Press, 2014
All rights reserved

First published 2014

Printed in China 5 4 3 2 1

KiDS ASTROLOGY™

LEO

23 July–22 August

CAMILLA GRACANIN

ABOUT KiDS ASTROLOGY

What is astrology?
Astrology is a big word that means 'finding answers in the sky'. People have been looking to the sky for answers for thousands of years.

What are star signs?
Star signs are a popular way that people use astrology today. There are 12 star signs. Each star sign or, more correctly, a sun sign, relates to the position of the sun at the time of someone's birth. Everyone has a star sign ... even you!

Why explore your star sign?
Which star sign you are depends on when you were born. People with the same star sign might have similar ideas and similar ways of thinking, feeling and experiencing life.

Exploring our star signs can help us to understand how and why we do things the way we do. We can discover a lot of information about ourselves and our many talents and special qualities too!

Are you on the cusp?
If your birthday falls on a date near the beginning or end of a star sign, you are on the 'cusp', or 'edge'. As the day the sun moves from one star sign to the next changes from year to year, it is helpful to read both the star signs closest to your birthday.

ARE YOU A LEO KID?

If your birthday is between 23 July and 22 August, you must be a Leo kid, like me!

Hi! I'm a Leo kid!

Kids with a Leo star sign are very creative, confident and energetic. They love being the leader, and are great at organising other kids.

Leo kids like to be the best. This means they can sometimes be quite competitive, but they always try to be generous and encourage their friends.

Leo kids are popular and cheerful. They are usually the kids who are invited to all the parties. They are very confident, and love being the centre of attention. Warm, loving and affectionate, they win friends wherever they go.

Leo kids are born to be the boss! Whether they are playing a game indoors or are out in the world, Leo kids like to take charge and be the leader. Listening to other kids is something they might need to work on, but Leo kids know how to make things happen.

Leo kids love to create drama, show off and be noticed. They have lots of creative and bright ideas. Most of the time their ideas will work and make people happy, but sometimes things don't go to plan.

Leo kids are eager to please, and they love receiving praise from their family and friends. When they feel they are not receiving enough praise or attention, they can become very unhappy.

Sometimes Leo kids need to remember that their loved ones cherish them, and that they don't need anyone to help them feel confident.

More about Leo

Each star sign has a symbol, ruling planet, element, gemstone, flower and colour linked to it. Leo kids have their own special things linked to their star sign.

Symbol: lion
Ruling planet: Sun
Element: fire
Gemstone: ruby
Flower: marigold
Colour: orange

ABOUT YOUR STAR SIGN FRIENDS!

AQUARIUS KIDS are clever, friendly, unique, inventive and determined, but can sometimes be stubborn and unpredictable.

20 January–19 February

PISCES KIDS are imaginative, creative, sharing, friendly and sensible, but they can sometimes be dreamers and unreliable.

20 February–20 March

ARIES KIDS are confident, adventurous, full of energy and are often good leaders, but they can sometimes be cheeky, pushy and impatient.

21 March–20 April

TAURUS KIDS are honest, hardworking, practical and loyal, but they can sometimes be lazy, stubborn and bossy.

21 April–20 May

GEMINI KIDS are entertaining, playful, honest, funny and quick-thinking, but they can sometimes be restless, nervous and picky.

21 May–21 June

CANCER KIDS are thoughtful, kind-hearted, protective, caring and sensitive, but can sometimes be moody, cautious and unconfident.

22 June–22 July

VIRGO KIDS are helpful, caring, sensitive, organised and practical, but can sometimes be critical, fussy and worriers.

23 August–23 Septem

LIBRA KIDS are charming, fair, thoughtful, easygoing and sociable, but can sometimes be indecisive, needy and easily influenced.

24 September–23 October

SCORPIO KIDS are determined, curious, affectionate, loyal and caring, but can sometimes be stubborn, distrustful and secretive.

24 October–22 November

SAGITTARIUS kids are cheerful, positive, funny, honest and adventurous, but can sometimes be over-excitable, restless and needy.

23 November–20 December

CAPRICORN KIDS are hardworking, practical, sensible, independent and organised, but can sometimes be worriers, shy and intense.

21 December–19 January

COLLECT THEM ALL!

Find out more about star signs and your friends by reading the other books in the Kids Astrology™ series.